SPOTLIGHT ON A FAIR AND EQUAL SOCIETY

ALLIES WORK TOGETHER

SHANNON H. HARTS

PowerKiDS press

Published in 2023 by The Rosen Publishing Group, Inc.
2544 Clinton Steet, Buffalo, NY 14224

Copyright © 2023 by The Rosen Publishing Group, Inc.

All rights reserved. No part of this book may be reproduced in any form without permission in writing from the publisher, except by a reviewer.

First Edition

Editor: Greg Roza
Book Design: Michael Flynn
Interior Layout: Rachel Rising

Photo Credits: Cover, fstop123/iStock.com; pp. 1–32 tavizta/Shutterstock.com; pp. 4, 18, 19 Monkey Business Images/Shutterstock.com; p. 5 LightField Studios/Shutterstock.com; p. 6 Ollyy/Shutterstock.com; p. 7 mentalmind/Shutterstock.com; p. 9 Prostock-studio/Shutterstock.com; p. 11 astarot/Shutterstock.com; p. 13 Fsch/Shutterstock.com; p. 14 CGN089/Shutterstock.com; p. 15 SergeiShimanovich/Shutterstock.com; p. 16 kenary820/Shutterstock.com; p. 17 https://commons.wikimedia.org/wiki/File:Sen._Bill_Bradley_(D-NJ)_in_his_office.jpg; p. 20 https://commons.wikimedia.org/wiki/File:Marche_pour_le_climat_27-09-2019_(Montr%C3%A9al)_14.jpg; p. 21 oneinchpunch/Shutterstock.com; pp. 23, 25 TextureWorld/Shutterstock.com; p. 23 Abraham Lincoln papers: Series 1. General Correspondence. 1833-1916: The Liberator, Friday, April 01, 1864 (Newspaper); p. 25 University of Maryland, College Park, MD; p. 27 https://en.wikipedia.org/wiki/File:Jeannette_Rankin,_Bain_News_Service,_facing_front.jpg; p. 29 https://commons.wikimedia.org/wiki/File:Martin_Luther_King_Jr_and_Matthew_Ahmann.jpg; p. 30 Mind Pixell/Shutterstock.com.

Library of Congress Cataloging-in-Publication Data

Names: Harts, Shannon H, author.
Title: Allies work together / Shannon H Harts.
Description: Buffalo, NY : Rosen Publishing, [2023] | Series: Spotlight on
  a fair and equal society | Includes index.
Identifiers: LCCN 2022028035 (print) | LCCN 2022028036 (ebook) | ISBN
  9781538388334 (library binding) | ISBN 9781538388303 (paperback) | ISBN
  9781538388341 (ebook)
Subjects: LCSH: Social justice. | Anti-racism.
Classification: LCC HM671 .H367 2023 (print) | LCC HM671 (ebook) | DDC
  303.3/72--dc23/eng/20220617
LC record available at https://lccn.loc.gov/2022028035
LC ebook record available at https://lccn.loc.gov/2022028036

Manufactured in the United States of America

Some of the images in this book illustrate individuals who are models. The depictions do not imply actual situations or events.

CPSIA Compliance Information: Batch #CWPK23. For further information contact Rosen Publishing, New York, New York at 1-800-237-9932.

CONTENTS

WHY ARE ALLIES IMPORTANT? 4
WHAT IS SOCIAL JUSTICE? 6
BECOMING AN ALLY 8
ALLIES WORK TOGETHER 10
LIGHTS IN THE WINTER NIGHT 12
BECOMING AN ANTIBULLYING ALLY 14
ALLIES IN SCHOOL 16
LEARNING ALLY SKILLS 18
ALLIES FOR ENVIRONMENTAL JUSTICE 20
HISTORIC SOCIAL JUSTICE ALLIES 22
WORKING TOWARD WOMEN'S SUFFRAGE 24
ALLIES FURTHER ADVANCE WOMEN'S RIGHTS 26
CIVIL RIGHTS MOVEMENT ALLIES 28
BE AN ALLY WHO SHAPES A BRIGHTER FUTURE 30
GLOSSARY 31
INDEX 32
PRIMARY SOURCE LIST 32

CHAPTER ONE

WHY ARE ALLIES IMPORTANT?

Allies ride the school bus. They sit with a new kid who everyone else avoids. Allies are not bystanders. When other kids are pushing someone's books out of their hands and knocking them all over the floor, allies get involved and take action. They stop and help if their neighbor's dog runs away. Allies often make the difference between meeting a goal and falling short. They share values and purpose. They can be strangers or friends. They can be next door or on the other side of an ocean.

Neighbors can be valued allies when storms harm homes and neighborhoods.

The people of Ukraine have allies all over the world. People welcomed those fleeing war. They opened their homes and public spaces to provide shelter and food. The people of Mayfield, Kentucky, became allies in rebuilding a town destroyed by a tornado.

CHAPTER TWO

WHAT IS SOCIAL JUSTICE?

According to the National Council for the Social Studies, "In a just society, every person would be of equal worth and value." Each person would have their basic needs met. They would be safe and secure. They would reach the goal of becoming a fully capable and contributing member of society.

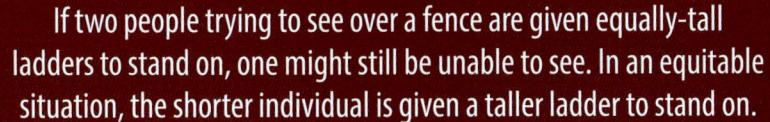

If two people trying to see over a fence are given equally-tall ladders to stand on, one might still be unable to see. In an equitable situation, the shorter individual is given a taller ladder to stand on.

In your life experiences, social justice is a goal. Working toward that goal is a responsibility for all citizens. How could your world be changed if every person were treated with equal worth and value? Fair access to opportunities, resources, and human rights would make that happen. What if the needs of individuals and groups were provided with respect for all differences? What if every child grew up with the chance to reach their **potential**? Perhaps **equity** could insure that. Everyone can be a force in the changes needed to achieve social justice.

CHAPTER THREE

BECOMING AN ALLY

Being an ally may be a response to something you see, hear, or experience during day-to-day life. You make a decision to speak up, act, or just to be on someone's side in a difficult moment. Being an ally can simply involve showing respect and understanding to someone who is different from you. **Empathy** can be a wake-up call for allies. They must make a choice to care instead of to ignore. Their values **motivate** them to do what is needed and what is right. Allies take a risk for a good reason. Working together, allies have the strength of many.

Being an ally often starts with listening and learning about the problems that other people face. Then it's important to stand up or act to create changes that can help those facing these challenges.

CHAPTER FOUR
ALLIES WORK TOGETHER

If you want to find allies working together, you don't have to look very far. Some are strangers, but working together they may become heroes and friends.

Nurses and doctors who cared for patients during the COVID-19 **pandemic** worked together in the face of risk and hardship. Firefighters and emergency responders may be allies to all in the community. Food pantry **volunteers** are allies to hungry people and families. People who **donate** blood and even organs like kidneys save lives and help people. Members of Team Rubicon, an organization of military veterans, travel and help communities affected by disasters. Kids who help elderly neighbors with grocery shopping and snow shoveling are allies. Sometimes people help cancer patients to get to their treatments and wait to take them home. Can you name more?

Search and rescue teams put themselves in danger to help people in need. They are true allies.

CHAPTER FIVE
LIGHTS IN THE WINTER NIGHT

Alliances may surprise the people who need them. They can give the gift of empathy through acts of courage and kindness. During the winter holiday Hanukkah, many people who practice the Jewish religion put a candleholder with nine candles, called a menorah, in their window. One year in a town, someone threw a rock into the window where a family had placed their menorah. The next night, every neighbor on the street had a menorah in their window, no matter what their religion. These allies defied hate with a simple gesture. More than that, they stood up for a fair and equal society in which everyone has the right to feel safe and respected.

This is a true story. Can you think of ways that allies working together can stand for kindness instead of hate, caring instead of bullying?

Allies can be strangers who let you know that you are not alone.

CHAPTER SIX

BECOMING AN ANTIBULLYING ALLY

Being an ally doesn't have to involve saving the planet. There are smaller things you can do. There are likely people you know who have been bullied for being different. Standing up for them can make you an ally.

To be an ally to those experiencing cyberbullying, you can avoid passing along harmful messages. Save proof of cyberbullying on a personal device. You can report it to social media platform leaders.

However, it can be hard to know what to do if you notice bullying. Bullying can be in person or online via mean comments on Instagram, TikTok, or other social media platforms. Often one of the best first steps is just to support the person being bullied. It's important to show empathy and take the time to understand the situation from their point of view. You can also say something simple to the bully, such as "Hey, that's not cool, cut it out." If the bullying doesn't stop or gets worse, it's important to tell an adult you trust, such as a school counselor.

CHAPTER SEVEN

ALLIES IN SCHOOL

Students just like you are working toward the goal of a fair and equal society. In New York State, in one big central school, many students who stood out because of their culture, social class, clothing, ethnicity, or other traits were often treated with mean words and physical harm. Some groups of students would not socialize with other groups. As in many schools, the cafeteria tended to be divided into tables where only certain groups could sit or be comfortable.

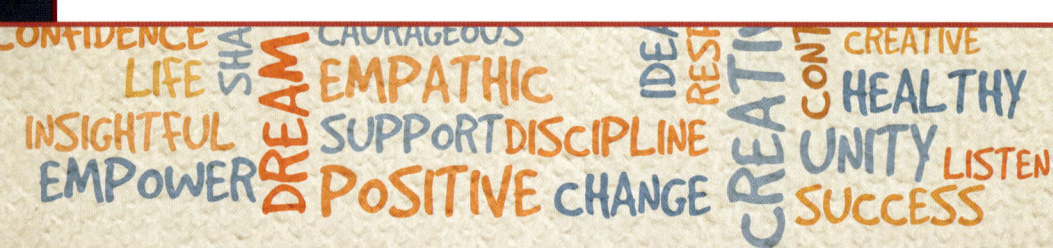

BILL BRADLEY

Bill Bradley—former professional basketball player and U.S. senator—once said: "Respect your fellow human being, treat them fairly...work together for a common goal and help one another achieve it."

Hundreds of students formed a Respect Club to change their school. For 20 years, students found amazing ways to break down barriers, stop violence, shine a light on all kinds of talents, and talk about differences as assets. Some students walked others who were in danger to and from classes. They pledged to be allies and changed their world.

CHAPTER EIGHT
LEARNING ALLY SKILLS

Being an ally can be challenging. It requires certain skills. Learning those skills starts with a goal of positive change. Many schools and groups turn to trainers like the National **Coalition** Building Institute to teach these skills. One program the coalition offers to elementary and middle schools is called "Welcoming Diversity: Building a Caring School Environment." It trains staff, parents, and students on how to be allies.

Skills for allies include nonviolent ways to respond to bullies, prejudice, and even **interpersonal** violence.

    A coalition created like this can have many **diverse** volunteers committed to working together. They learn how to respond to **prejudice**, build relationships, stop violence, and be leaders. Sharing and listening to stories and **testimony** about unjust or unfair experiences, a core team becomes very aware of the problems they need to solve. They also learn about how much even very diverse people have in common. Small steps toward action build confidence in new skills. Larger steps follow.

CHAPTER NINE

ALLIES FOR ENVIRONMENTAL JUSTICE

Climate change is causing the usual weather around the world to get worse. Those who are economically and socially **disadvantaged** are at the greatest risk from climate change's impact, which includes air pollution, deadly heat waves, increased wildfires, and rising sea levels.

In 2015, Greta Thunberg was 12. She became an ally in a movement to change human activities causing climate change. She protested outside of a government building in Sweden and inspired thousands of other students to take action.

GRETA THUNBERG

Climate activists often fight for environmental justice, which means everyone has the same safeguards from harmful economic actions and pollution.

Mari Copeny, at the age of 8, met then-U.S. President Barack Obama after writing him a letter about the deadly water problems and shortages in her hometown of Flint, Michigan. Mari was already organizing and raising awareness about harmful lead in her city's water.

CHAPTER TEN
HISTORIC SOCIAL JUSTICE ALLIES

Long before the term "ally" meant someone working towards social justice, many citizens in the United States took action to work against injustice. This included a journalist named William Lloyd Garrison. Garrison had a hard life growing up in the early 1800s, but he didn't let this stop him from finding success. When he was just 13, Garrison became an apprentice with a newspaper publisher.

Garrison knew that, because he was white, no part of his life was nearly as hard as it was for the more then 3 million Black enslaved people in the United States. He started a newspaper called the *Liberator* that called for an end to slavery. He decided to take these efforts even further by starting an organization called the American Anti-Slavery Society. By 1840, it had around 150,000 members! Many others also fought for social justice and abolishing slavery.

CHAPTER ELEVEN
WORKING TOWARD WOMEN'S SUFFRAGE

The Thirteenth Amendment to the U.S. Constitution ended slavery in 1865 following the bloody Civil War. The amendment bars states from denying "equal protection of the laws" and the right to vote because of race. At the time, the Constitution also lacked rights for women, and many women saw this as an opportunity.

A New York woman named Elizabeth Cady Stanton made a bold move in the summer of 1848. She organized a meeting of 300 men and women in Seneca Falls, New York, to create a Declaration of Sentiments. It was like the Declaration of Independence, but it listed the rights that women should have as U.S. citizens. This began the U.S. women's rights movement. In 1851, Stanton met Susan B. Anthony, a powerful ally. Thousands and thousands of allies soon joined the movement.

> At first, the women's rights movement included many goals, such as giving women equal access to jobs and the right to own property. However, it narrowed to focus on suffrage, or the right to vote, after the Civil War.

MARYLAND Suffrage News

Vol. IV, No. 19 *AUGUST 7, 1915* *Five Cents*

A GOVERNMENT OF THE PEOPLE BY THE PEOPLE FOR THE PEOPLE

ARE NOT THE WOMEN HALF THE NATION?

CHAPTER TWELVE
ALLIES FURTHER ADVANCE WOMEN'S RIGHTS

Anthony and Stanton worked hard to convince Congress to add rights for women to the Fifteenth Amendment. In the end, it gave citizenship to Black men without giving any rights to women. However, the movement continued to grow. In 1911, thousands of marchers took to the streets of New York City for the second New York Suffrage Day Parade. About 150 male allies marched alongside the thousands of women. These men were mocked by members of the crowd, but they kept going. After nearly another decade of **activism**, in 1920, the Nineteenth Amendment finally gave women the right to vote.

In the 1960s and 1970s, there were many efforts to expand women's rights in work and family life. A man named Richard Graham became an ally by working to enforce the Title VII Act, which forbid employment **discrimination** based on sex.

Jeannette Rankin, the first woman elected to the U.S. Congress, not only worked to make women's suffrage possible but also to gain better health care for women and babies.

CHAPTER THIRTEEN
CIVIL RIGHTS MOVEMENT ALLIES

In the late 1800s, many lawmakers worked to pass state and local laws to limit the rights of Black Americans. These were called Black Codes and Jim Crow laws. They required Black Americans to use separate public facilities. They also limited the kinds of jobs Black people could have and the property they could own.

In 1955, a Black woman named Rosa Parks was riding on a public bus in Montgomery, Alabama. When the white bus driver ordered her and others to give up their seats for white passengers and move to the back of the bus, she refused and was arrested. This sparked the Montgomery bus boycott, led by Dr. Martin Luther King Jr. It began the U.S. civil rights movement. White Jewish attorney Stanley David Levison became one of King's close advisers and allies. Hundreds of thousands of allies stood up and took action for civil rights.

Like Stanley Levison, Mathew Ahmann, shown here with Martin Luther King Jr., was an important ally for the civil rights movement. He used his role as a Catholic Church representative to gain support.

CHAPTER FOURTEEN
BE AN ALLY WHO SHAPES A BRIGHTER FUTURE

Without the work of activists and allies, the world would be a different place today for many people facing injustice, unfairness, and inequity. People are taking action to create a more just world. They're taking a stand against violence toward others. And thousands of students worldwide are standing up for climate change action.

There are many ways you can help as an ally. You can stand up to someone who is being a bully, show empathy to someone who is different, and be a leader in your school or community. Pay attention to fairness and equity and organize others to work for change. No matter your social justice interest, your individual skills and ideas can help create a better world.

GLOSSARY

activism (AAK-tuh-vih-zum) Acting strongly in support of or against an issue.

coalition (koh-uh-LIH-shuhn) An alliance of distinct parties, people, or states for joint action.

disadvantaged (dis-ad-VAN-tehjd) Lacking in the basic resources or conditions believed to be necessary for an equal position in society.

discrimination (dih-skrih-muh-NAY-shun) Different—usually unfair—treatment based on factors such as a person's race, age, religion, or gender.

diverse (duh-VUHRS) Having many different types, forms, or ideas.

donate (DOH-nayt) To give as a way of helping people in need.

empathy (EHM-puh-thee) Being aware of and sharing someone else's feelings.

equity (EH-kwuh-tee) Freedom from bias or favoritism.

interpersonal (ihn-tuhr-PUHR-suh-nuhl) Being, relating to, or involving relations between people.

motivate (MOH-tuh-vayt) To provide with a reason for doing something.

pandemic (pan-DEH-mihk) An outbreak of a disease that occurs over a wide geographic area and typically affects a significant proportion of the population.

potential (puh-TEN-shuhl) An ability or quality that can lead to success or excellence.

prejudice (PREH-juh-diss) An unfair feeling of dislike for a person or group because of race or religious or political beliefs.

testimony (TEHS-tuh-moh-nee) A statement made by a witness under oath especially in a court.

volunteer (vahl-uhn-TEER) Someone who does something to help because they want to do it.

INDEX

A
Ahmann, Mathew, 29
American Anti-Slavery Society, 22
Anthony, Susan B., 24, 26

B
Bradley, Bill, 17

C
civil rights movement, 28, 29
Civil War, 24, 25
climate change, 20, 21, 30
Congress, U.S., 26, 27
Constitution, U.S., 23, 24
Copeny, Mari, 21
COVID-19, 10

D
Declaration of Sentiments, 24

E
empathy, 8, 12, 15, 30
environment justice, 21
equity, 7, 30

F
Fifteenth Amendment, 26

G
Garrison, William Lloyd, 22, 23
Graham, Richard, 26

J
Jim Crow laws, 28

K
King, Martin Luther, Jr., 28, 29

L
Levison, Stanley David, 28, 29
Liberator, 22, 23

M
Montgomery bus boycott, 28

N
Nineteenth Amendment, 26

P
Parks, Rosa, 28

R
Rankin, Jeanette, 27

S
Seneca Falls, 24
slavery, 22, 23, 24
Stanton, Elizabeth Cady, 24, 26
suffrage, 24, 25, 26, 27

T
Thirteenth Amendment, 24
Thunberg, Greta, 20

PRIMARY SOURCE LIST

Page 23
Issue of the *Liberator*. Newspaper. April 1, 1864.

Page 27
Jeanette Rankin. Photograph. February 27, 1917. By Bain News Service.

Page 29
Martin Luther King Jr. and Mathew Ahmann. Photograph. August 28, 1963.